FOOD IN THE CIVIL WAR ER

A Selection of Recipes

Adapted from the Original Nineteenth-Century Texts,

Brought Up-to-Date for the Modern Cook

Books in the American Food in History Series

A Selection of Modernized Recipes from

FOOD

IN THE CIVIL WAR ERA

THE SOUTH

EDITED BY HELEN ZOE VEIT

Adapted by Jennifer Billock

Michigan State University Press

EAST LANSING

♾ The paper used in this publication meets the minimum requirements
of ANSI/NISO Z39.48-1992 (R 1997) (Permanence of Paper).

Michigan State University Press
East Lansing, Michigan 48823-5245

Printed and bound in the United States of America.

21 20 19 18 17 16 15   1 2 3 4 5 6 7 8 9 10

Library of Congress Control Number: 2015933882
ISBN: 978-1-61186-167-9 (pbk.)
ISBN: 978-1-60917-454-5 (ebook: PDF)

Cover and book design by Erin Kirk New

Cover illustration is from Isaac Pim Trimble, *A Treatise on the Insect Enemies of
Fruit and Fruit Trees* (New York: W. Wood and Co., 1865), frontispiece, Michigan State
University Special Collections.

Michigan State University Press is a member of the Green Press Initiative and is
committed to developing and encouraging ecologically responsible publishing practices.
For more information about the Green Press Initiative and the use of recycled paper in
book publishing, please visit www.greenpressinitiative.org.

Visit Michigan State University Press at www.msupress.org

CONTENTS

A selection of recipes, updated and tested by food editor
Jennifer Billock, from

Food in the Civil War Era: The South, edited by Helen Zoe Veit
(ISBN 978-1-61186-164-8)

✳

Introduction

The antebellum South was nothing if not agricultural. In fact, thanks to its vast farmlands, mild weather, and massive, enslaved workforce, the antebellum South was one of the most productive agricultural regions in history. On the eve of the Civil War, as white Southerners contemplated their prospects in the conflict, few imagined their agricultural system would be anything but an asset. After all, Southern cotton was the fuel driving the Industrial Revolution. But Southerners overestimated the power of cotton and underestimated the power of food. Before the war, the South had imported a significant portion of food from outside the region, including much of their pork, beef, wheat, potatoes, cheese, and butter. Once the war started, the inadequacy of Southern food production quickly became obvious. The Union blockade of Southern ports reduced imports of food and other materials to a trickle, and the blockade only tightened as time went by. Even when some farmers were able to grow surplus food, they often didn't have any way to send it to market because much of the Southern transportation network—never

comprehensive to start with—was commandeered or destroyed in the war. Southerners' inability to produce adequate food or to move the food they had where it was needed contributed directly to their defeat.

Wartime food shortages affected home life as much as military strategy, and recipes from the time give a sense of how concretely the war changed what Southerners ate. But the war didn't affect all Southerners equally. On the home front, wealthy Southerners often maintained a buffer against privation, while poorer Southerners were much more likely to suffer. Poor Southern women whose husbands and other male family members left to fight for the Confederacy often became so desperate for food and other basic resources that they begged the men to return and help them. As conditions worsened across the South, women's inability to keep their families afloat by themselves seriously undermined the Confederate war effort. But the people who were by far the poorest and who suffered the most were the four million Southerners—a third of the population—who had been enslaved. The war took a devastating toll on

This is an abridged version of the introductory essay "Seeing the Civil War South through Its Recipes," in *Food in the Civil War Era: The South* (East Lansing: Michigan State University Press, 2015).

Southern African Americans, with hunger, exposure, and displacement contributing to staggering rates of sickness and death.[1] Money and race created gross differences in the ways Southerners experienced the war, protecting some from true want while exposing many others to the harshest deprivations and suffering. But no Southerners were unaffected by the war, and the experiences of the war—and in particular the increasingly romanticized memories of those experiences—profoundly shaped Southern cuisine.

Nineteenth-century Southern cookbooks teem with the kinds of recipes we expect to find when we go looking for Southern food: grits, gumbo, succotash, Hopping John, catfish, coleslaw, watermelon pickles, chitterlings, sweet potato pie, and many, many more. It's not a coincidence that Southern cuisine has a strong identity or that that identity is roped to the Civil War era.

Many nineteenth-century cooking techniques were really forms of preservation. Jams, vinegars, alcohols, pickles, smoked meats—these were all ways to extend the life of perishable foods. Before reliable refrigeration, preserving food was crucial to survival.[2] But here's what's interesting about the prevalence of preserved foods in cookbooks from the Civil War era: many of the flavors we associate with Southern cuisine today are really the flavors of preservation, from the bite of vinegary peppers to the sticky sweetness of fruit syrups to the pungency of pickles to the burn of homemade liquors to the saltiness of sausage. What's even more interesting is that, at the time, the flavors on Northern tables wouldn't have been much different. Preservation techniques were ubiquitous in kitchens across the country by necessity. Meanwhile, other cooking techniques we associate with Southern cuisine weren't at all exclusively Southern, either. For example, when we think of a mess of limp collards or green beans boiled down to a savory heap with salt pork, we think of them as uniquely Southern dishes. But people were boiling vegetables to death all over the United States in the mid-nineteenth century. In large part, that was because many people believed they had to cook vegetables for hours to make them digestible.

The point is that many of the flavors we associate with Southern cuisine today are really the flavors of the nineteenth century, *not* necessarily flavors that were unique to the South. Why is that? A big reason is that people have been nostalgically celebrating the cuisine of the "Old South" ever since the end of the war, and as a result, Southern cuisine hung on to many nineteenth-century cooking techniques—and continued to value the tastes and textures that resulted—in a way Northern cuisine did not. And for that matter, "Northern cuisine"? It hardly seems to exist. If somehow the war hadn't happened—if there'd never been an "Old South" versus a "New South"—Southern cuisine might not exist either. It certainly would have been very different because there would have been no reason to canonize the tastes and techniques of this particular era.

As it was, nostalgia for antebellum eating began before the war was even over. Already by the early 1860s, Southern women like Maria Barringer and Annabella

Hill were at work on cookbooks memorializing prewar cooking styles. And when they were finally published in the late 1860s, both of their cookbooks would fondly recreate "war" recipes, too.[3] Other cookbooks soon appeared devoted explicitly to the cuisine of the "Old South." One of the best and most accurate of these is the 1881 *What Mrs. Fisher Knows about Old Southern Cooking*. Unlike many of the racist books that would be published in later decades by white authors claiming to recreate plantation cookery, this book was written by a formerly enslaved South Carolina woman named Abby Fisher who had migrated to California with her family after the war.

Enslaved African Americans were central to the development of Southern food but not in the ways later imagined in racist fantasies about faithful slave cooks.[4] The origins of the Southern cuisine canonized in the decades after the Civil War are complex, including a "cross-pollination" of European, Native American, and African ingredients and cooking techniques.[5] Southern cuisine is particularly tied to African cuisines. Many enslaved Africans arrived in the American South with knowledge of farming, herding, and cooking techniques, valuable skills that shaped what people in the South grew and how they ate it.[6] As the slave trade diffused West African crops around the Atlantic world, foods like rice, okra, yams, and black-eyed peas became staples in Southern kitchens and dining rooms, along with indigenous ingredients from the Americas like corn, tomatoes, sweet potatoes, peanuts, squash, and beans.[7]

As with all cuisines, in fact, the borders of Southern cuisine get messy when you look closely because ingredients and recipes moved around all the time. By the mid-nineteenth century, Southern recipes like gumbo were appearing regularly in Northern cookbooks, just as some Southerners regularly cooked from Northern cookbooks. And like all cuisines, Southern cuisine changed over time, according to the shifting availability of ingredients, the development of new cooking tools, and changes in fashion or taste. This volume includes recipes excerpted from seven sources: five formally published cookbooks, Confederate periodicals published during the war, and a never-before-published handwritten culinary manuscript. Together, they give a sense of how diverse, complex, and surprising Southern cuisine was in the era of the Civil War.

HELEN ZOE VEIT

BREAKFAST

Sweet Potato Waffles

PREP TIME: *5 minutes; Cook time: 10 minutes;*
Total time: 15 minutes

MAKES 8 4-INCH WAFFLES

INGREDIENTS

4 tablespoons peeled, cooked, mashed sweet potatoes

2 tablespoons sugar

2 tablespoons butter, melted

2 cups wheat flour

1¾ cups milk

STEPS

Mix all the ingredients together.

Grease a preheated waffle iron with cooking spray.

Pour the batter on in ½ cup dollops and cook according to the manufacturer's directions.

❊ Marmalade Peach

PREP TIME: *25 hours; Cook time: 5 hours;*
Total time: 30 hours

MAKES 2½ CUPS

INGREDIENTS
2 pounds peaches (about 5 large)
2 cups sugar

STEPS
Peel and cube the peaches. Discard the peels and the pits.

Put the peaches in a deep dish. Sprinkle the sugar thickly over the peaches. Refrigerate overnight.

The next morning, mash everything together thoroughly and pour the mixture into a pot. Do not add water.

Cook over medium-low heat for 5 hours, stirring occasionally. The finished marmalade will be more like syrup.

Store the marmalade in a covered container in the refrigerator. It will thicken as it cools.

Eggs and Potatoes

PREP TIME: 1 hour, 20 minutes; Cook time: 10 minutes; Total time: 1 hour, 30 minutes

SERVES 4

INGREDIENTS

6 medium potatoes

⅛ teaspoon salt, or to taste

⅛ teaspoon pepper, or to taste

3 eggs

3 egg yolks

4 tablespoons butter

Pepper to taste

STEPS

Boil the potatoes until they are fork tender (about 20 minutes). When completely cool, peel them and cut them into small pieces. Sprinkle salt and pepper over the potatoes and set aside.

Whisk together the eggs and the egg yolks and set aside.

Melt the butter in a skillet and add the potatoes. Cook over high heat until the potatoes are browned and heated through. Stir in the eggs and mix until they are set. Remove from heat.

Season with pepper to taste and serve immediately.

Mrs. J.'s Receipt for Scotch Hash

PREP TIME: *15 minutes; Cook time: 30 minutes;*
Total time: 45 minutes

SERVES 4

INGREDIENTS

2 pounds cooked corned beef (preferably leftover,
   slightly dry)

1 small white onion

1 teaspoon cayenne pepper

1 tablespoon butter

1 cup hot water

4 eggs

STEPS

Preheat oven to 400°F.

Mince the corned beef and put it in a skillet. Chop
the onion and add to the skillet. Add the cayenne,
butter, and water. Cook on medium heat until very hot
throughout. Remove from heat.

Beat the eggs together in a 9-inch pie pan. Stir in the
meat mixture. Bake for 30 minutes or until set.

Serve immediately.

✳ Fried Egg Plant

PREP TIME: *15 minutes; Cook time: 10 minutes; Total time: 25 minutes*

SERVES 4

INGREDIENTS
1 large eggplant
6 tablespoons salt
½ tablespoon pepper
¼ cup flour
3 tablespoons butter

STEPS
Cut the top and bottom off one large eggplant. Discard the ends. Cut the eggplant into half-inch round slices. Lay the slices flat and cover them with a thick layer of salt, about ½ tablespoon per slice. Let sit for 5 minutes. This will remove the bitter taste from the eggplant.

Wash the slices in cold water to remove the salt and pat them dry with a paper towel. Lay them flat again and sprinkle the pepper over the slices. Dip each slice in flour to coat both sides.

Melt the butter in a skillet and fry each slice over medium-high heat until golden brown on each side. Add more butter as needed.

Serve immediately.

LUNCHEON

❋ A Nice Twelve O'Clock Luncheon

PREP TIME: *10 minutes; Cook time: 2 minutes;*
Total time: 12 minutes

MAKES 8 TOAST TRIANGLES

INGREDIENTS
2 2-ounce tins anchovy fillets
4 slices multigrain bread
1 cup chopped parsley
2 cups shredded white cheese, such as mozzarella
3 tablespoons butter, melted

STEPS
Turn on the broiler.

Drain the tins of anchovies and set the fish aside.

Lightly toast the bread and cut in half on the diagonal. Put 2 or 3 anchovy fillets on each toast triangle. Place the toast pieces on a broiler-safe dish.

Mix together the parsley and cheese. Sprinkle over the toast pieces until covered well. Pour the melted butter evenly over each piece.

Put the toast pieces under the broiler for 2 minutes, or until golden brown and bubbly. Serve immediately.

Scalloped Oysters

PREP TIME: *25 minutes; Cook time: 25 minutes;*
Total time: 50 minutes

SERVES 4

INGREDIENTS

6 eggs

4 8-ounce cans of oysters

1⅔ cups bread crumbs, divided

¾ teaspoon pepper, divided

3 tablespoons butter, divided and cut into quarters,
   plus 2 tablespoons butter, melted

¾ teaspoon salt, divided

STEPS

Preheat oven to 350°F.

Hard-boil the eggs. When cool, peel them and cut them
into slices.

Butter a deep 6x8-inch casserole dish.

Drain the oysters. Put a layer of oysters in the
casserole dish, then a layer of sliced eggs. Cover with
⅓ cup breadcrumbs. Sprinkle on ¼ teaspoon pepper.
Place 1 tablespoon quartered butter pieces over the
layer. Sprinkle on ¼ teaspoon salt. Repeat in this
fashion until all the oysters are in the dish. Use 1 cup
bread crumbs for the last layer. Drizzle the melted
butter over the top.

Bake for 25 minutes.

✳ Very Fine Corn Muffins

PREP TIME: *25 minutes; Cook time: 20 minutes;*
Total time: 45 minutes

MAKES 18 MUFFINS

INGREDIENTS
1 tablespoon vegetable shortening
2 cups cornmeal
2½ cups water
6 eggs
1 teaspoon salt

STEPS
Preheat oven to 400°F.

Using your hands, mix together the vegetable shortening and cornmeal.

Boil the water and stir in the cornmeal mixture. Remove from heat and put the mixture into a stand mixer with a dough hook. Stir on low speed until lukewarm, stopping periodically to scrape the sides of the bowl. The dough will be very stiff at this point. (Alternatively, knead mixture by hand until cooled, about 15 minutes.)

Meanwhile, beat the eggs and salt together. Pour the egg mixture into the cornmeal mixture and stir until just combined. Switch to the whisk attachment and mix until thoroughly combined, stopping periodically to scrape the sides of the bowl.

Grease a muffin pan and drop the batter by rounded tablespoons into the cups. Bake for 20 minutes or until the muffins are puffed and bounce back at the touch.

Let cool. If desired, serve with butter or honey.

 Cucumbers

PREP TIME: *1 hour, 15 minutes;*
Total time: 1 hour, 15 minutes

SERVES 4

INGREDIENTS
2 large cucumbers
1 medium white onion
2 teaspoons salt
1 teaspoon pepper
¼ cup white vinegar

STEPS
Peel the cucumbers and cut them into thin, round
slices. Put the slices in a bowl of cold water and let
them sit for 1 hour.

Once the cucumbers are in the water, peel and slice the
onion. Put the onion in a separate bowl of cold water
and let them sit for the remainder of the hour.

Drain all the water from both bowls and mix the
cucumber and onion together in a large bowl. Add in
the salt, pepper, and vinegar. Toss and serve.

 # Mint Cordial

PREP TIME: *24 hours, 10 minutes;*
Total time: 24 hours, 10 minutes

MAKES A 5-CUP PITCHER

INGREDIENTS

1½ ounces fresh mint

1½ cups plus 1 quart whiskey

1 cup sugar

STEPS

Remove the stems from the mint and lay the leaves in a shallow lidded container. Pour 1½ cups whiskey over the mint. Cover the container and refrigerate for 24 hours.

Strain the whiskey and discard the mint leaves. Pour the whiskey into a pitcher and add the remaining quart and sugar. Mix until the sugar is dissolved.

Serve in cordial glasses, with ice if desired.

DINNER

Jumberlie—A Creole Dish [Jambalaya]

PREP TIME: *45 minutes; Cook time: 35 minutes;*
Total time: 1 hour, 20 minutes

SERVES 8

INGREDIENTS

1 small whole chicken

1 cup white rice

4 14.5-ounce cans diced tomatoes, or 6 large tomatoes,
   blanched and diced

1 pound honey ham steak, diced

1 teaspoon salt

1 teaspoon pepper

STEPS

Cut the chicken into ½-inch chunks, being sure to separate all the joints and remove as much skin as possible. Do not remove bones from the legs or wings; discard the ribcage. Put the chicken into a large stockpot.

Add the rice, tomatoes (including juice), ham, salt, and pepper. Mix well.

Bring to a boil over high heat, then reduce heat to medium-low heat and cook, stirring occasionally, for 35 minutes or until chicken reaches an internal temperature of 165 degrees.

Cheese Biscuit

PREP TIME: *15 minutes; Cook time: 20 minutes;*
Total time: 35 minutes

MAKES 16 BISCUITS

INGREDIENTS
½ pound cheddar cheese, grated
3⅓ cups flour
½ pound butter, melted
Salt to taste

STEPS
Preheat oven to 400°F.

With your hands, mix together the cheese, flour, and butter until thick enough to roll. If the dough is too dry, add butter in tablespoon increments.

Roll out on a lightly floured surface to ½-inch thickness. Cut into 2-inch squares and place on a lightly greased cookie sheet.

Bake for 20 minutes or until firm to the touch and golden brown. Salt to taste.

✳ Corn Oysters

PREP TIME: *45 minutes; Cook time: 6 minutes;*
Total time: 51 minutes

SERVES 8

INGREDIENTS
10 small ears of corn
2 eggs, beaten together
2 tablespoons flour
¼ teaspoon salt
¼ teaspoon pepper
⅛ cup milk
2 tablespoons butter

STEPS
Cut through the grain on the corn, slicing each kernel
open but leaving it on the cob. Scrape down the side
of the cob with a spoon to remove the pulp. This will
be a messy process; it might help to put down a cloth.
Reserve the pulp in a bowl. It should make about
4 cups of pulp.

Add the eggs, flour, salt, pepper, and milk to the pulp
and mix well.

Melt the butter into a skillet over medium heat.
Drop in tablespoons of the corn batter and fry until
golden brown on both sides.

Serve immediately.

❋ Spinach

PREP TIME: *5 minutes;* Cook time: *5 minutes;*
Total time: 10 minutes

SERVES 8

INGREDIENTS

8 cups water

2 tablespoons salt

2 pounds spinach

2 tablespoons butter, melted

1 tablespoon white vinegar

Pepper to taste

STEPS

Mix the water and the salt and bring to a boil. Add the spinach. Cover and cook over medium-high heat until the spinach is tender, about 3 to 5 minutes.

Drain the water and press out any excess from the spinach.

Transfer the spinach to a bowl and pour the butter and vinegar over it. Pepper to taste.

Serve as a side or on its own with poached eggs on top.

 # Ochra

COOK TIME: *12 minutes; Total time: 12 minutes*

SERVES 8

INGREDIENTS
2 cups water
4 cups okra
2 tablespoons butter, melted
2 tablespoons white vinegar
⅛ teaspoon salt
⅛ teaspoon pepper

STEPS
Bring the water to a boil over high heat. Add the okra and return the water to a boil.

Reduce the heat to medium. Cover and cook for 10 minutes, stirring once halfway through.

While the okra cooks, whisk together the butter, vinegar, salt, and pepper.

Drain the okra and toss in the butter dressing. Serve immediately.

✳ Egg Plant

PREP TIME: *25 minutes; Cook time: 6 minutes;*
Total time: 31 minutes

SERVES 4

INGREDIENTS
2 large eggplants
3 egg yolks
1 cup bread crumbs
¼ teaspoon salt
¼ teaspoon pepper
4 tablespoons butter

STEPS
Cut off the stems and bottoms of the eggplants.
Submerge them in boiling water for 5 minutes.
Remove eggplants from the water, and when they're
cool, cut them into 1-inch-thick round slices. Do not
peel. Set aside.

Whisk the egg yolks together. Put the bread crumbs in
a separate dish.

Dip the eggplant slices into the yolk, then into the
bread crumbs, covering completely. Season each side
with salt and pepper.

Melt the butter in a skillet over medium heat. Add the
eggplant slices and fry them until golden brown on
each side.

❋ To Make Pickle-Lily

PREP TIME: *10 minutes; Total time: 10 minutes*

MAKES 2 1-QUART JARS

INGREDIENTS

Assorted vegetables for pickling
6 cups white vinegar
2 tablespoons salt
1 teaspoon peppercorns
1 teaspoon whole allspice
1 teaspoon whole mace
½ teaspoon whole cloves

STEPS

Heat the vinegar over medium heat until very hot, but do not let it boil.

Remove from heat and add the salt, peppercorns, allspice, mace, and cloves. Divide the mixture into jars.

Store the jars in the fridge and add whole or sliced vegetables. (Vegetables were pickled as they came into season.) Cucumbers, radishes, green beans, and onions work well with this recipe.

DESSERT

 # Blackberry Pie

PREP TIME: *10 minutes; Cook time: 45 minutes;*
Total time: 55 minutes

MAKES 1 9-INCH PIE

INGREDIENTS

1 package two-piece premade pie crust, or *Pastry for*
  Making Pies of All Kinds (recipe below)
4 cups blackberries, divided
5 tablespoons brown sugar, divided
1 tablespoon flour, divided

STEPS

Preheat oven to 375°F.

Line a pie plate with the bottom crust. Put in a layer of berries, then a layer of brown sugar, then a dusting of flour. Repeat until the pie plate is full. Heap the berries a little in the center and add a splash of water if desired.

Put on top layer of crust and pinch the edges together. Cut a slit in the center of the top crust.

Bake for 45 minutes, or until golden brown and bubbling.

❋ Sweet Potato Pudding

PREP TIME: *30 minutes; Cook time: 1 hour; Resting time: 15 minutes; Total time: 1 hour, 45 minutes*

MAKES 1 9X13-INCH CASSEROLE

INGREDIENTS

1 pound sweet potato

6 eggs, beaten together

2 cups powdered sugar

1½ cups butter, melted

1 teaspoon nutmeg

Half a lemon

1 cup brandy

1 tablespoon sugar

STEPS

Preheat the oven to 350°F.

Peel and cube the sweet potatoes. Boil them until very tender and mash them.

Mix together the eggs, powdered sugar, butter, nutmeg, and brandy. Grate ¾ of the lemon peel into the mixture. Add the potatoes. Stir until combined and pour into a greased 9x13-inch casserole dish.

Bake for 1 hour, then remove the dish from the oven and let it sit for 15 minutes.

Sprinkle sugar over the top and garnish with a few strips of lemon peel.

❋ Cocoanut Pie

PREP TIME: *1 hour, 30 minutes; Cook time: 40 minutes;*
Total time: 2 hours, 10 minutes

MAKES 1 9-INCH PIE

INGREDIENTS

1 whole coconut

½ cup powdered sugar

1 tablespoon butter

1 tablespoon vegetable shortening

4 egg yolks

4 egg whites

1 lemon

¼ cup sweetened condensed milk

1 premade pie crust, or *Pastry for Making Pies of*
   All Kinds (recipe below)

STEPS

Preheat oven to 400°F.

Using a hammer and nail, poke two holes in the
coconut. Drain the juice into a bowl. Strain it through
cheesecloth and reserve the liquid.

Wrap the coconut in a towel and hit it with a hammer
around the middle until it cracks in half. Put the halves
into the oven and bake for 20 minutes or until the shell
breaks away from the meat. Do not turn off the oven.

When the coconut has cooled, pry the meat out by
sticking a butter knife between the shell and meat. It
should pop out easily. Carefully peel the interior rind
from the coconut with a vegetable peeler and rinse
the meat.

Grate the coconut meat into a bowl and pour the reserved liquid over top. Add the powdered sugar, butter, and vegetable shortening. Cream together in a stand mixer. Mix in the egg yolks and the grated rind and juice from the lemon.

In a separate bowl, beat the egg whites until small peaks form. Add them to the coconut mixture and combine. Pour in the sweetened condensed milk and mix together.

Line a pie plate with crust and pour in the coconut mixture. Bake for 40 minutes, or until firm in the middle.

❋ Pastry for Making Pies of All Kinds

PREP TIME: *10 minutes; Total time: 10 minutes*

MAKES ENOUGH PASTRY FOR 1 PIE

INGREDIENTS

1⅓ cups flour

1 tablespoon butter

1 tablespoon vegetable shortening

½ cup water

STEPS

Mix all the ingredients together with fingers until the dough is able to be rolled. It will be very pliable, like pizza dough.

Roll out the dough to ¼-inch thickness for immediate use, or store in the freezer.

WAR RECIPES

 # Panola

---

PREP TIME: *40 minutes; Total time: 40 minutes*

MAKES 4 CUPS

INGREDIENTS
½ teaspoon vegetable oil
1 cup dry corn

STEPS
Lightly coat a skillet with the oil, wiping any excess with a paper towel.

Add corn to the skillet. Cover and cook over medium heat, shaking skillet frequently, for 30 minutes or until popped. While popcorn will fully pop, regular dried corn will swell and pop about halfway.

Put the popped corn into a food processor and grind to a powder. Sift it and then regrind the bigger pieces.

Once completely ground, season the corn with either salt to taste or cinnamon and sugar to taste.

✳ Rye as a Substitute for Coffee

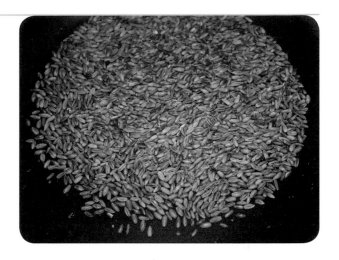

PREP TIME: *10 minutes; Cook time: 5 minutes; Total time: 15 minutes*

MAKES 5 CUPS

INGREDIENTS
¼ cup dried rye berries

STEPS
Toast the rye berries in a dry pan over high heat, stirring frequently, until browned. Some of the berries may pop.

Remove the rye from heat and grind it in a coffee grinder until powdery.

Put the rye in a coffee filter and brew according to 6-cup coffee machine directions. A French press can also be used with a coarser grind. The finished coffee will be light in color and mild in taste.

✳ Substitute for Cream in Tea or Coffee

PREP TIME: *5 minutes; Total time: 5 minutes*

SERVES 1

INGREDIENTS

1 egg white

½ teaspoon butter, softened (omit if using for tea)

STEPS

Beat the egg white until frothy. Stir in the butter until dissolved.

Temper coffee into the egg white mixture to avoid curdling and stir well.

Serve immediately.

✳ "Cornfed" Cake (war)

PREP TIME: *5 minutes;* Cook time: *50 minutes;*
Total time: 55 minutes

MAKES 1 8X8-INCH CAKE

INGREDIENTS
½ pound butter, melted
8 eggs
2 cups sugar
1½ cups cornmeal
1 teaspoon baking soda

STEPS
Preheat oven to 350°F.

Mix all the ingredients together and pour into a
greased 8x8-inch baking dish.

Bake for 50 minutes, or until set and dark golden-
brown. Serve with butter or honey, if desired.

 # Potato Pudding (war)

Prep time: *5 minutes; Cook time: 1 hour;*
Total time: 1 hour, 5 minutes

Makes 1 9-inch casserole

Ingredients

1 cup sweet potato, cooked and mashed

1 cup cornmeal

2 cups sugar

1 cup buttermilk

½ teaspoon baking soda

Steps

Preheat oven to 350°F.

Mix all the ingredients together and pour into an ungreased 9-inch casserole dish.

Bake for 1 hour, or until a toothpick inserted in the center comes out clean.

Serve immediately.

NOTES

1 Jim Downs, *Sick from Freedom: African-American Illness and Suffering during the Civil War and Reconstruction* (Oxford: Oxford University Press, 2012).

2 See Jonathan Rees, *Refrigeration Nation: A History of Ice, Appliances, and Enterprise in America* (Baltimore: Johns Hopkins University Press, 2013).

3 Diary of Maria Massey Barringer, Barringer Family Papers, Mss 25884, Shirley Small Special Collection, University of Virginia. I'm indebted to Christopher Farrish for passing along this source.

4 McElya argues that stories of enslaved people's affection and devotion for their masters were "designed to provide reassurance that their author's patriarchal benevolence was real." Micki McElya, *Clinging to Mammy: The Faithful Slave in Twentieth-Century America* (Cambridge: Harvard University Press, 2007), 4.

5 Damon Lee Fowler, "Annabella Powell Hill," in John T. Edge, ed., *The New Encyclopedia of Southern Culture*, vol. 7: *Foodways* (Chapel Hill, University of North Carolina Press, 2007).

6 Judith Carney, *In the Shadow of Slavery: Africa's Botanical Legacy in the Atlantic World* (Berkeley: University of California Press, 2009), 2, 105.

7 Carney, *Shadow of Slavery*, 107.

More Civil War–era recipes—as well as descriptive essays that provide a unique portrait of Northern life via the flavors, textures, and techniques that grew out of a time of crisis—can be found in:

Food in the Civil War Era: The North
Edited by Helen Zoe Veit
Cloth, 215 pages
ISBN 978-1-61186-122-8

AND

A Selection of Modernized Recipes from
Food in the Civil War Era: The North
Adapted by Jennifer Billock
Paper, 48 pages
ISBN 978-1-61186-156-3